WILDERNESS SOJOURN

WILDERNESS SOJOURN

Notes in the Desert Silence

DAVID DOUGLAS

1817

Harper & Row, Publishers, San Francisco

New York, Grand Rapids, Philadelphia, St. Louis,
London, Singapore, Sydney, Tokyo

Library of Congress Cataloging-in-Publication Data

Douglas, David.
  Wilderness sojourn.

    1. Spiritual life—1960–   2. Wilderness
(Theology)   3. Douglas, David.   I. Title.
BV4501.2.D647 1987   242   86-45803
ISBN 0-06-061993-7

89 90 91 92 93 MCN 10 9 8 7 6 5 4 3 2 1

To Deborah

CONTENTS

ACKNOWLEDGMENTS

In a book extolling solitude, it may seem incongruous to list so many names, but I am beholden to people who have read the manuscript and offered invaluable comments. In particular, I want to thank Annie Piper, Nancy Arnon, Richard Holland, Steve McDowell, Bud Redding, Ken Hunt, John Piper, Ree Sheck, Don Lemons, Cindy Quicksall, David Quicksall, and, most of all, my wife Deborah Douglas for her clarity, understanding, and encouragement.

From the first time I saw canyons of southern Utah—as a fourteen-year-old with my family from Washington, D.C.—through hiking days at the Colorado Rocky Mountain School, and later with members of Santa Fe's Sierra Club, I've gone into wilderness nearly as often with others as I have gone alone. I've been extraordinarily fortunate to hike with such companions, to have shared their experience and insights as we ventured into corners of America's surviving wildlands.

I want to express my appreciation to Rebecca Laird at Harper & Row for her kindness and support in working to make this book possible.

First Presbyterian Church in Santa Fe has provided a wellspring of community and challenge, and I'm grateful to the congregation and to the Revs. Jim Brown, Rob Carlson and Tom Truscott.

And finally, I want to add a word of hope that my daughters, Katie and Emily, will someday encounter for themselves the wilderness and other sanctuaries of stillness.

First Day

It is late afternoon in the desert, and I am following the curves of a shallow gully through the sand. Here only a sinuous wrinkle in the landscape, the gully will soon begin to deepen, its soft sides giving way to rock cliffs. Friends have been to this corner of the American Southwest before me, and they have spoken of passages in the desert—narrow canyons of rose-red stone—that wind for miles to meet a wilderness river. Before dusk settles in, I hope to be in one of these canyons, setting up camp in the sand under a blizzard of stars. I am alone, and no sound except my footsteps breaks the silence of the desert.

Far behind me I have left my car in a grove of cottonwood trees. I will not be returning for several days. I feel anxious, as I always do at this point of departure, not only for my own safety but the car's as well—that it be here upon my return, unvandalized, able to transport me home from the wilderness.

The afternoon is warm and windless, with the sun slanting into my eyes as I walk. Except for some piñon jays flying down to assess their chances for food, the desert is empty and still.

If asked, "Why go into the wilderness?" I tend to speak about the landscape and its colors and wildlife. My response is filled with figures: the number of miles I've walked, mountains I've climbed, or wild creatures I've counted.

But once I actually enter wilderness, I am more honest with myself. The lure is less what I can tally or photograph than what I can sense: the quiet, intangible qualities of desert, mountain, and forest.

Wilderness has been characterized as barren and unproductive; little can be grown in its sand and rock. But the crops of wilderness have always been its spiritual values—silence and solitude, a sense of awe and gratitude—able to be harvested by any traveler who visits.

With each hour I walk, the canyon grows deeper, its walls soon rising far over my head. The cliffs hang like tapestries, their crevices spun with wildflowers. A shallow stream has begun to flow along the canyon floor and, as I follow it, I find myself doing what I rarely do during daylight hours: praying. Normally my prayers are dutiful and diffuse, part of an absentminded ritual offered up on the rim of sleep. But here they have an urgent clarity: "God be with me," I say in advance of any perils I might encounter.

"Pray without ceasing," St. Paul advised. These early hours in wilderness suggest to me how that improbable charge might indeed be possible.

If someone years ago had suggested that a wilderness sojourn could be a religious retreat, I would have objected:

retreats, in my mind, took place under a roof—at conference centers or monasteries or urban contemplative houses.

But my view was constricted. There could be other separations from daily regimens, other withdrawals into reflection and silence. And all that, I was slow to see, could take place in the open air, in an arena of stone and sand.

At least in theory. This first afternoon in the canyon, I am preoccupied with an avalanche of secular concerns: what to cook for dinner, how to avoid snakes, where to sleep for the night. Aside from prayers for my safety, my thoughts are disjointed, my perspective myopic. To grace these early hours as a "retreat" seems presumptuous. This is a backpack trip that aspires to be a retreat.

Twilight. The hour of the day I feel most keenly the distance I've come. I could not leave this place and return to my car even if I desired. Not enough light remains to guide me; I would turn an ankle in the first mile if I tried. I am committed to this corner of the world until daybreak.

For the night's camp I have found a terrace of hard sand, and I begin to set up a small tent I have carried with me. I tell myself this will provide protection against bad weather. But the night is mild; not a cloud can be seen. No, the tent will be for my mind. I erect its thin nylon fabric as a wall of security against the darkness.

I begin the nightly ritual, shaking out my sleeping bag, anticipating a scorpion but finding, as usual, only stray grains of sand. I lay out beside me a panoply of belongings for the night—canteen, flashlight, watch, handkerchief. I position each one carefully. I am never more fastidious than I am here in the wilderness. Rather than having to lurch to find these talismans if jarred from sleep, I put them within reach. Dawn seems distant; awakening in the tent will be disorienting enough. I create around me a space of predictability and control in this setting where there is so little of either.

Before entering the tent, I sit for a few minutes on a sandstone ledge. With no canopy of clouds to trap the day's heat, the desert is quickly cooling. Two stars emerged moments ago; when I glance up again, a thousand more have rushed to join them.

I pull on a sweater and take up a pen. On a piece of paper I choose words that approach what I have begun to feel. I write, without elaboration: "Awe . . . exhiliration . . . disquiet . . . reverence." The words seem pale and inadequate in the last light of day. All they really do is skirt the edges of this peculiar emotion: a feeling that is, at heart, simply a shuddering sense of dependence on God. And that is why I have come.

Second Day

I awaken not long after dawn and lie in my sleeping bag. Thomas Merton, chronicling his premonastery life, once lamented all the lost mornings that he had slept through—something there was no danger of doing as a monk. Or, I might add this morning as I shift a shoulder blade to avoid a pebble, as a backpacker.

The sun has not yet climbed the surrounding cliffs and the canyon is suspended in a quivering salmon-pink light. In a few hours all this will change. The canyon will become a white-hot cauldron—its plants and animals seemingly wilted, its colors blanched. But now the extraordinary light gives a rich, warm texture to the cliffs and the wet stream rocks. Slender cottonwoods fringe the watercourse, and their leaves are drenched in as deep a shade of green as I have seen.

The reflected light of morning is the canyon's equivalent of dew—fresh, cleansing, forgiving. This is the time of day when all efforts that lie ahead seem possible, when all promises to God seem as though they can be kept.

The sand is cold under my feet as I dress. I eat breakfast—a fresh orange, oatmeal cookies, coffee—while standing beside the stream. Hearing a faint rumble, I look up to see a plane's contrail arcing through the sky. I have a friend who talks wistfully of traveling to Alaska to find wilderness. To him, only the north country's impenetrable isolation promises to exclude contrails or distant vibrations of machinery.

My friend's version of wild country is intensely personal. Other definitions abound, but wilderness has at heart always seemed subjective. Its boundaries can be fluid, shifting with each individual. For me, wilderness depends not only upon the terrain and wildlife but upon one other quality: my vulnerability. Is this the setting where I feel less self-sufficient, more conscious of my reliance on God?

I cannot draw this theological definition of wilderness on a map, but as I travel in the open air I can sense when suddenly the threshold of wilderness is being crossed.

To my side, the stream, a resolute sculptor of the canyon, polishes away at the rim of a small waterfall. A trail climbs around the cataract and I follow it past tiers of layered rocks. The broken stones offer ideal shade for a snake. Each step I take places my ankles inches away from the dim recesses.

I walk cautiously, my ears straining for warning rattles, my eyes scanning the rocks ahead. I am alert for any shift in shadow. My adrenal glands are functioning properly.

Suddenly a lizard darts across my path and scurries into a nearby crevice, leaving its tail protruding and my respiration impaired. I move faster now, relieved to see the trail at last swing back down beside the stream. Entering the water with a series of quick breaths, I rest on a boulder and look behind me.

A curious phenomenon: if I had crossed that last stretch of trail with companions, my anxiety—had I even been conscious of a threat—would have been minimal.

But I am alone this morning, and that makes all the difference.

With no one else around for miles, this solitude makes me conscious—almost exaggeratedly so—of the canyon's pitfalls. When I have traveled in backcountry with friends, I have felt insulated from the terrain and its risks. The footfalls of companions produce a soothing effect.

But to enter the wilderness invariably accompanied by others can be like camping at dusk with a lantern. Comfort and security are provided, but the surroundings are kept well at bay. We are turned inward, enclosed in a tight circle of light. Only if we momentarily relinquish the lantern does the night begin to appear with stars and shapes and silhouettes, stretching out limitlessly with unnerving beauty.

The honing, clarifying solitude of these first days is particularly sharp-edged; it has been more than a year since I have been so utterly alone.

The first time I withdrew alone to backcountry, years ago, I had been prepared for having only the sinews stretched, not the soul as well. Prayer was the most unexpected gift of wilderness. I was unfamiliar with the writings of the early desert Christians; I had skimmed unseeing over any references to prayer made by naturalists and explorers.

Prayers in the wilderness were like streams in the desert to me—something unanticipated and unchronicled welling up, and because of that surprise, appreciated all the more. Not until I actually left the wilderness was I conscious what had been the extent of my thirst.

The canyon is narrowing. Rarely wider than a stone's throw, the sides now appear to fuse together just ahead. Only gradually, as I continue walking, can I discern an opening between the walls, a hint of the corridor that winds on into the desert. Part of the lure of canyon travel is this sense of seeing only so far ahead, of watching massive cliffs appear to part before one's eyes as one barely shifts perspective.

There is much that can go wrong in this narrow passage. One could be caught in a storm, struck by lightning, injured by rockfall. But for the most part, the prospect of peril looms larger than any actual danger. A traveler can walk thousands of desert miles without twisting a knee or glimpsing a rattlesnake.

It is precisely the uncertainty, the possibility of peril, the distance walked away from electric lights and hospitals that is the value of wilderness. We do become apprehensive. Our well-being is precarious. We briefly enter an arena where illusions of self-sufficiency come unraveled. And

it is in this state that we are inclined to turn to prayer, to listen to someone beyond ourselves.

I should not have found it so startling that prayer could flourish here, that the physical uncertainties of wilderness could make a visitor spiritually receptive. There are, after all, biblical precedents, the Moses-led Sinai wandering being a single epic example. For forty years the ancient Hebrews sojourned in the desert, receiving from God their daily bread. Pieces of manna awaited them each day on the desert floor—a portion for each person, but impossible, save over the Sabbath, to store. When the Hebrews attempted to hoard it, the manna rotted. God's stated purpose? To instill in the generation raised in the wilderness a sense of complete, and daily, dependence on God alone. Delusions of self-sufficiency fared poorly in the Sinai.

Toward noon I stop for lunch, my sack of food in bulging contrast to the Hebrew's spare flakes of manna. As I eat I spread out a map of the canyon on the sand. The map is mainly a diversion. Unlike travel in the mountains or forests, travel in narrow canyons offers few chances to get lost. With water flowing to one side, a visitor has only two options, upstream or downstream. The current provides an unerring compass.

An overhanging ledge blocks the sun, evenly separating the floor of the canyon into light and shadow. I will finish my meal with some chocolate, waiting until the sun begins to intrude upon my shade, then continue downstream.

Images of the Sinai keep recurring to me here. With its burnt sand and sullen granite, the terrain could never have been confused with the land of milk and honey. But like this desert canyon, neither was it a region only of heat and unremitting harshness. Tucked away in its folds, the Sinai harbored pastures, oases, and running water. In the desert, God's protective shadow could be felt each day. During the Sinai years, the law was given and the covenant was renewed. In no other setting did the Hebrews see so clearly their relationship to God. They encountered "grace in the wilderness," as Jeremiah wrote: "I remember thee, the kindness of thy youth, the love of thine espousals, when thou wentest after me in the wilderness. . . ."

The enduring problem in the Sinai was the wandering of the heart. We tend to confuse wilderness with the tribulation itself, instead of seeing it as the setting where the real tribulation could be overcome.

Wilderness has drawn humans closer to God throughout history. Why should we, in the twentieth century, believe this is suddenly no longer true? Long after the Exodus, in a time of recurring apostasy, Hosea spoke of God wishing to "allure" the people back into the wilderness yet again—this time to the parched hills beyond Jericho. There, wrote the prophet, God would "speak tenderly" to them.

The verse suggests almost a divine yearning, particularly so as "speak tenderly" also translates as "speak to the heart." There on the familiar stage of stone and sand, the wilderness would once again serve as an instrument of reconciliation, and God's people would respond "as they had in the days of their youth."

Reinhold Niebuhr once warned that technological achievements "have beguiled us into a false complacency. We have forgotten the frailty of man." Most of us recall that frailty only in the throes of personal crisis or tragedy. But other events can puncture pride, and travel through the daunting terrain of wilderness has been such an event for stiff-necked peoples of all generations.

Seen from the passenger planes that regularly cross this corner of the Southwest, the landscape about me takes on a leaflike pattern: the main canyon stem I've been following lined on both sides by smaller branching canyons. I keep turning up these tributaries, for they have their own beauty as secretive places, less traveled, with richer hints of elusive wildlife.

They also hold the promise of tapering into cracks so thin a visitor must turn sideways to pass through. I came upon one on a spring day once: a fissure hundreds of feet deep and only a yard wide, as though the blade of an enormous knife had been slowly, sinuously drawn through peach-colored stone. Only when the sun was directly overhead could light enter in shafts; more often it glanced off the walls as it fell, rendering the bottom of the passageway as luminous as the inside of a conch shell.

The light washed over surreal stonework—shapes of whale fins, eagle beaks, and giants' fists—emanating from the wall. Some stretches of the canyon had been caressed into wavelike peaks and troughs, the walls appearing to flow like pulled taffy.

I climbed into one of these alcoves hidden below the desert and, looking about me, wondered when it was in the past millennium that wind, sand, and water had ceased to abrade and instead—all three together as God's instruments—had begun to sculpt.

A friend uses nature to express an aspect of his faith. He holds an apple and asks, "How can anyone look at such a perfectly designed and packaged fruit and deny that there's a Creator?" He can also see God's handiwork in cultivated fields and in the shade trees of his front lawn.

But his appreciation of divine craftsmanship stops short of wild country. "Wilderness," he says, "frightens me."

For my friend, an apple is a window to God; for others, wilderness provides that window. The temptation seems to be to close, uncomprehending, each other's window.

Around each bend of the canyon I look for an evening campsite. Just before dusk I find what I have been searching for—a stretch of soft sand with a spring nearby.

While deliberating whether I need the tent tonight, I begin a meal of soup, crackers, and dried beef. My hunger is still slight now in these early stages of the trip; my body is adjusting to the sudden wrenching away from a sedentary workday. I am profoundly thirsty, however, and I drain a quart of water mixed with iced tea crystals while preparing dinner. The sky has shaded from a pale lavender to a charcoal dusk by the time I finish eating. Lamps are just going on in distant city parks. I am a child of some of those parks, and I would suspect that fear born there —of urban muggings and rapes—has helped to curdle the feelings of many people toward wild country. Every assault in a city park conveys the image of nature not only as harboring the sinister but as somehow unleashing it. If Central Park with its police patrols and electric lights holds such menace after dark, what must the heart of wilderness be like?

I walk down to the water's edge and fill my canteen. As the stream sluices through bedrock, the sound reverberates off the high cliffs. "Silence" is at times a misnomer for the offering of wilderness. Tonight, in addition to this full-throated stream, I can hear the cadence of crickets and a shuffle of wind through the leaves.

But each sound has its place, its own reassuring rhythm. Until later in the dark, that is, when I hear an unexplained rustle in the bushes or slither of stones down an embankment. In the middle of the night, the silence of wilderness becomes, invariably, not silent enough.

Long ago, after my first travels in wilderness, I was inclined to assume it was God who had moved; that God somehow revealed himself more clearly in desert and mountain. Only with reluctance did I conclude that any moving had been done by me. "As soon as a man is fully disposed to be alone with God," noted Thomas Merton, "he is alone with God, no matter where he may be—in the country, the monastery, the woods or the city."

Wilderness has never been the only stage where God, in Hosea's words, "speaks to the heart." It is just that there, in the shattering stillness, some have been more inclined to listen.

Tonight as I lie in a sleeping bag, my back forms a shallow depression in the soft sand. A few yards away, the tent stands erected should I decide later to climb inside; I am too weary to move right now.

Last night, through the tent's nylon, the sky appeared only as a luminous blur. This evening I can almost believe the claim I doubted as a child—that there are more stars in the sky than grains of sand in all the seashores of the world.

When I was younger, our family would step outside the house after dinner and see overhead, instead of constellations, only a dull orange glow—like some encapsulating dome—from the city's prodigious electrical output. "The heavens are telling the glory of God," wrote the Psalmist, "and the firmament proclaims his handiwork." The city's night sky might have given the Psalmist pause.

I now live where stars are not such strangers, yet when I am home I rarely consider them. As I shuttle between my house and car for evening meetings, it is too cold or late to do more than hastily glance upward. But here, flat on my back, a rolled-up sweater for a pillow, I watch stars for hours. My eyes take in the whole throbbing night sky. When the time finally comes to rest, I cannot do so in this position: my eyes refuse to shut and to close out the shooting stars and candescent constellations. To sleep, I roll on my stomach, turning my back to the night sky as it blazes away in silence until dawn.

THIRD DAY

This morning the sun slanting over the rimrock awakens me—a reveille that has me up and walking downstream while the canyon is still in fragrant shadows.

Accompanied by matinal trills of a canyon wren, I move briskly past glens of green willows backlit by the sun. Around one bend, however, I find myself stopping in midstride. Just ahead of me, morning light pours like honey hundreds of feet down the cliff, flooding the stone, filling each crevice. The lower reaches of the cliff, still sunk in shadow, sweep down to where hanging gardens of maidenhair fern and crimson wildflowers wreathe a freshwater spring.

This sudden pausing in midstep has happened to me before in wilderness, usually at dawn or dusk, when an encounter with color, light, and shadow has left me transfixed. I find myself breaking into applause, the cliffs magnifying the sound of my clapping. Someone standing on the canyon rim high above me would hear the incongruous sound—a measure of gratitude for the creation—drifting up from this crack in the earth before it was carried away on a current of desert wind.

What I find distinct about gratitude in wilderness is its simplicity—the thankfulness I feel here is for what I usually take for granted: my capacity to breathe, move, and see. At times I've felt flashes of gratitude during a harrowing moment: while descending a ridge before lightning struck, or finding my way after being lost. But for the most part, gratitude here wells up unexpectedly, in the quiet corners of the day, over events small and ordinary: chancing upon a sun-washed cliff, or catching a stray scent of sage.

Gratitude is the other side of dependence on God: to take anything for granted in the wilderness seems presumptuous, blasphemous. And so, here in these naves of vaulting stone, prayers of thanksgiving begin to edge out prayers of petition.

This morning I walk beside groves of tamarisk bushes, their green featherlike branches tipped at the ends with purple blossoms. These plumes are gentle reminders to me of how short-lived gratitude can be.

The tamarisk thrives not only in these canyons but in the Sinai as well. It may have been the source of the Hebrews' manna. (The tamarisk's gum, when consumed by insects, can be secreted to the ground as edible flakes that taste like honey.) But as the Exodus narrative makes clear, any appreciation felt by the Hebrews changed before long to grumbling. They soon disparaged their daily bread as "this worthless food."

I find that once I leave wilderness, the gratefulness I feel for simple gifts, here so resolute, begins to dissipate; I cannot store gratitude. When the sun rose in the Sinai, the honeylike flakes melted away. My sense of gratitude, I sometimes suspect, is as enduring as manna at high noon.

The canyon narrows for a stretch, and I can almost touch both sides at once. Far overhead, the cliffs pinch the sky to a ribbon of blue. Light falls here in shafts, and I can see, at the level of my eyes, mud caked on the walls—a testimony to the flash floods that have coursed through the canyon. A reminder that the perils of wilderness, while rare, are quite real.

In another canyon I saw a flash flood once, one that began as a roar and grew to shake the earth. A friend and I had been downstream, below camp, wandering up slender side canyons. We had strolled down ill-equipped, without matches, extra clothing, food, or flashlights. In a spectacular failure of memory, we had forgotten that though the day had been cloudless, a storm had raged the preceding evening. High up, in the mountains, the rains would be gathering in the rills all day, coalescing in the arroyos, and finally, turbid and swollen, soon be crashing through the deep rock canyons. And the flood came, just after we had returned and climbed to our camp in a cliff alcove. Five minutes earlier, passing through a steep-walled narrows, we would have been caught in the flood, in its early fury of tangled bushes, mud, and gray waters. But as it was, we were perched safely, and we sat on a ledge with our legs over the side and watched until the dark came and all that left was the sound and the stars and the feel of the earth trembling all night long.

I spoke with a friend about traveling through the desert, mountain, and forest. She listened for a time and then shook her head. "I don't know," she said. "I haven't felt a sense of dependence on God in those places. Where I have felt it is in the ocean, when I've been underwater—swimming or snorkeling—a sense of vastness, of my vulnerability, of having left behind the customary props. But the sea is different from what you're talking about, isn't it?" I replied no, I didn't think so; my perspective had just been limited. I was landlocked, a stranger to the ocean for the most part, and I had been drawing the boundaries of wilderness too narrowly.

As I walk this morning, I continue to be followed by the notes of a canyon wren. They fall in sweet staccato descent, vibrating for just a moment in this stone amphitheater. I rarely see the wrens; they stay out of sight, these cleft dwellers, hidden on high canyon ledges.

We are told that "not a sparrow is forgotten before God." An astonishing statement. I fight against a literal interpretation: surely there are too many sparrows—or canyon wrens—for that assurance to be true. I find it easier to acknowledge God's attention taking in each of the earth's humans, but I try to rein in divine providence when it comes to sparrows.

But the passage stands to be wrestled with. The verse, uttered to prove a separate point, can alter forever how we regard the singularity of the earth's creatures and, most important, how we regard the omniscience of God.

After a few hours of walking, I stop at a spring and fill the canteens, a task that takes some time as the flow emerging from a crack in the cliff is the width of a thread.

We say this earth is God's creation. The hymns we sing at church acknowledge it; the biblical passages read during services eloquently confirm it. God "calls the stars by name" . . . "gives life to all things" . . . "feeds wild beasts and birds" . . . "sends fruitful rain."

But I don't think we believe the words. We would act less recklessly if we did, not only in irreversible ecological affairs, but in quieter relationships with the earth and its creatures day to day.

We respond indifferently to so many other biblical affirmations, it's not surprising that "The Earth is the Lord's" has become a sentiment we attend to absentmindedly.

Looking about me, I can see that the wall across the way does not rise vertically, but rather slants gently to the canyon's rim, appearing to offer a rare route out of the canyon to the desert plateau above. In a few moments I've begun working my way up the slope. The ascent is even easier than I imagined, and before long I am coming out on top of the canyon.

I feel no need to explore, as I've been walking for hours. Instead, I find a slickrock dome and, scrambling the few feet to its summit, watch shadows spread over the undulating expanse of pink sand and stone.

I once visited another desert at this time of day, just

as shadows were stretching down to the Jordan River. There on the edge of the Judean Desert, I found myself wondering why it was that Jesus had been led into the wilderness. The usual answers—to encounter Satan (as though to beard the lion in his den) and to undergo temptation—suddenly seemed incomplete. For if the purpose had been to confront Satan, surely the meeting could have occurred elsewhere; as the incident at the Temple's pinnacle makes clear, it was not as though the devil's domain was restricted to wilderness. And if the purpose was to grapple with temptation, why couldn't this have begun immediately, rather than after the long prelude of forty days? I had always associated the Judean wilderness simply with the denouement, with Christ turning aside the temptations. But as I stood there on the edge of the maroon hills and ravines where Jesus fasted and prayed, I had another sense of the desert's role—less as a setting for temptation than as one for preparation.

To Bethlehem we go, countless pilgrims each year, to the town of Jesus' birth. In the crowds and noise we jostle each other as we glimpse the grotto, now adorned with votive candles and incense burners, where tradition has placed the manger. But why, along with this visit to the cradle of his birth, should there not be one as well to the cradle of his ministry—the Judean wilderness? To know for a few moments, on our own pilgrim skins, its dust and wind and heat. We can perhaps learn as much about the earthly man, the obstacles he faced, and the idea of God entering into space and time, by standing on the edge of those sunstruck hills as by crowding into a Bethlehem shrine.

Few scriptural passages are more familiar than those recounting Jesus' forty days in the wilderness. But languishing in disproportionate neglect are gospel accounts of other sojourns taken by Jesus into wild country: "And he withdrew himself into the wilderness and prayed"; "And . . . he went out into a mountain to pray, and continued all night in prayer to God"; "And when he had sent the multitudes away, he went up into a mountain apart to pray: and when the evening was come, he was there alone"; "And in the morning, rising up a great while before day, he went out, and departed into a solitary place and there prayed."

Even if I had never strayed from asphalt ways, I would like to think these passages would have given me pause. Why did Jesus withdraw to these lonely places beyond the outskirts of towns? And why did he go alone, leaving even the disciples behind? On these occasions, Jesus was not simply seeking a refuge from the crowds, though wilderness could provide such a sanctuary (as mentioned in John 6:15). Rather, Jesus was here using the desert and mountain for another purpose, one the gospel writers made explicit: prayer. The country beyond the edge of civilization was the setting Jesus chose for prayer. These verses provide more than topographic color or a bridge in the gospel narrative. They offer a clue to prayer and the way in which wilderness—both first-century Judean and twentieth-century American—can serve as a God-given house of prayer.

We read about these other sojourns and the accounts do not seem to affect us. The verses are rarely used during services; they seem to us to have little relevance to our lives. No other action of Jesus'—particularly one so frequently undertaken—is so widely slighted. But doesn't his decision to withdraw, to separate himself briefly from those around him, suggest that we too should consider physical retreats into solitude and prayer? Our agendas are no more urgent that his was. If Jesus in his startlingly brief ministry—no more than two or three years in length —could find time for this pattern of withdrawal and return, surely we too can occasionally follow a similar contemplative sequence. Retreating when we are able to a room, garden, or cabin. And not forgetting as well the setting that Jesus so often chose—the unsurpassed silence of lonely, windswept places.

Today, across this American desert, I can see a range of mountains wrapped in a plum-blue mantle of afternoon light; slender troughs of snow still glissade down the sides of the peaks. Years ago, before I knew much of the Bible, I remember borrowing a verse that appealed to me: "I will lift up mine eyes unto the hills, from whence cometh my help."

I took the words by themselves, standing stark and

bare, and I have seen them used since, isolated in a similar fashion on calendars and notecards. The suggestion I drew was that the landscape itself—the stolid massifs and soaring pinnacles of stone—girded the soul.

I had, of course, overlooked some alternative punctuation: "I will lift up mine eyes unto the hills. From whence cometh my help?" I, and others, had pulled a verse from its context, blurring the distinction between creator and creation. More important, the musings of the Psalmist were woefully incomplete without the addition of the next verse, which I only adopted with time: "My help comes from the Lord, who made heaven and earth."

Below me now, the canyon is gathering in the dusk; parts of the stream catch reflected light and from up here the canyon floor appears to cradle braided currents of silver. Time to be off, to collect the canteens I left down at the spring and to make an early camp in the twilight.

The evening is still and windless. I've camped on a shelf of sandstone above the water. An intervening ledge muffles even the stream's whisper. Tonight, if one listened hard enough, one could hear stars emerging.

I rest on the ground, motionless and bone-weary. I should pitch the tent, but everything in my body urges me to sit and soak in the pool of silence. I realize how rare this quiet is in my life—an absence of activity, movement, or sound. Here the stillness of the wilderness imposes itself with an enveloping hush; a visitor eventually has little choice but to be internally quiet as well, and recall the Psalmist's words: "Be still, and know that I am God."

When I am home, in the city, I complain about distractions, yet surround myself with them: magazines, radio, newspapers, television. Hungry for news and entertainment, I often fill to overflowing the spaces of silence.

I've occasionally taken brief retreats to a monastery, but even there, with its hushed codes of silence, I am drawn to a diversion: the monastery has a bookstore, its shelves laden with titles I've yet to read by the Desert Fathers, Charles de Foucauld, Carlo Carretto, and other contemplatives. I walk out, arms full, carrying books and pamphlets and newsletters, so many words to read that I can delay indefinitely any confrontation with myself or God.

The simplicity of a wilderness retreat is decreed by necessity: I cannot carry with me an inordinate number of books. A thin volume or two, along with a miniature edition of the Bible, is all the weight my pack can accommodate.

Leaning against a ledge, I pull out the book I have brought with me for these days—C. S. Lewis's *Mere Christianity*. I don't read entire chapters tonight, but rather paragraphs here and there, pausing to take in the evening sky of glowing embers.

Just as there are foods such as lemons or salted crackers that taste appropriate in the desert, so there are books that are particularly satisfying here: reflections by C. S. Lewis and Simone Weil, Henri Nouwen and Thomas Merton. The authors' voices are clear, spare, and nourishing; what they counsel seems more accessible from the distance of this wilderness perspective.

Years after a journey, I can tell which paperbacks I have carried along. Their covers are wrinkled, their backs are bent, and, as I pull them off my bookshelves, grains of sand trickle down from their pages onto the rug.

I've often brought Lewis's *Mere Christianity* to the wilderness; in proportion to its weight I know of few volumes so lucid and wise. Lewis's insights enabled me, as they have others, to slip past obstacles I had erected to Christianity. But one morning not long ago, as I waited in a canyon alcove for a rain shower to end, one of Lewis's thoughts struck me as uncharacteristically facile. I was reading his recollection of an incident during one of his speeches. An individual in the audience had been critical of Lewis's strong emphasis on doctrine.

"I've no use for all that stuff," he had told Lewis. "But, mind you, I'm a religious man too. I *know* there's a God. I've *felt* Him: out alone in the desert at night: the tremendous mystery."

Lewis wrote that while he agreed with the man to a point, the "experience in the desert" was inadequate: doctrine and theological study were maps that provided further direction. But then the Oxford don added another, more troubling, line. "You see, what happened to that man in the desert may have been real, and was certainly exciting, but nothing comes of it. It leads nowhere."

I reread the last sentence: "It leads nowhere." I'm not so sure. For some, it can lead everywhere—to God and a sense of complete and continuing dependence on him. The "experience in the desert" can serve as a prelude to investigation—a triggering event of faith that impels one to venture on into doctrine. Lewis seemed to be skimming over an irony of our time: that preoccupation with doctrine and theological instruction has relegated the desert experiences to the primitivist heap. Much of the Judeo-Christian tradition was born in the wilderness. To neglect entirely that origin is to prune the tree's branches while forgetting to water its roots.

If scenery were all wilderness offered, the land would not need to be preserved or visited. Photographs could serve as adequate testaments for future generations. "Here child," we could say, turning pages, "these were what we called sequoias."

But pictures poorly convey intangible qualities of wild country. Wilderness is more than pleasing tableau glimpsed from afar. The stronger reason to value wilderness is what we feel when we actually visit it—no longer holding the landscape at arm's length but directly immersing ourselves in its silence, solitude, and awe. It is by donning walking clothes and stepping into wild country that we encounter these spiritual gifts.

I walk down to the stream to gather water for tomorrow's breakfast. Standing on the sandbank, I watch the current disappear around a bend. I am not far from this canyon's end. Tomorrow, God willing, I will follow this stone corridor to its junction with a wilderness river.

As I fill the canteens, I find myself thinking of my family. Are they well? What are they doing at this moment, as darkness settles into this canyon? I am nearly the farthest distance I will be from them on this journey, and their absence seems overpowering.

In the first days in wilderness, I tended to be preoccupied with my own well-being, but my thoughts are now being drawn back to the community I have left behind. Concerns about family and friends, jobs and avocations, take on a peculiar clarity in the dusk.

No distractions tonight, no diversions to occupy me. I find thoughts gradually transposing themselves into prayers. Yes, here in this passageway there is not a distraction in sight. Nothing to turn to. Nothing except God.

FOURTH DAY

This morning, not long after breaking camp, I round a bend and find myself in a shallow pool of quicksand. As I begin slowly to sink, I try with an adrenal surge to extricate myself, but the wet sandy clasp is quite firm. I temporarily reconcile myself to its embrace, uncertain which is more curious: the sensation of being pulled into the earth or the world around me rising.

The quicksand climbs no higher than my knees before abruptly stopping. A friend once, on her first journey to these western canyons, learned there was no record of anyone actually dying in quicksand, that one rarely sank above one's waist. Overcoming her initial caution, she found herself delighting in the sudden, deliberate descent, and went about looking for pools of quicksand to leap into.

But I have stumbled here inadvertently, and anxious to be on my way, I begin a concerted effort to free myself. Removing my backpack, I shift the weight of my legs, tugging up on one foot, then the other. At first I only work my way in deeper, my legs feeling as though they are going through a taffy pull. Then, gradually, as the pool belches and gurgles, I begin to emerge, my calves plastered with a glutinous coat of dripping sand.

Quicksand is a gentle reminder, I tell myself, as I sit on a nearby stone and refasten a tennis shoe: this uncertain, unsettled ground we travel through is not in the purely spiritual realm. If one's stride threatens to change to a strut, wilderness can always provide the heart-sinking pool of quicksand or the deflating blade of cactus.

For some time after my first travels in wilderness, I recoiled against using one word that came swiftly to mind: *fear.* The word conjured up a corrosive emotion to be avoided at all costs.

But I'm not so certain now. To fear is not unequivocally debilitating; there can be healthy, judicious, pride-puncturing fear. The Bible repeatedly advises one "to fear God," that "the fear of the Lord is the beginning of wisdom." Stirrings of fear for our well-being in wilderness—triggered by broken terrain and unknown wildlife beyond our ability to control—can lead inexorably to a sense of dependence on God.

A wilderness traveler walks through country so finely crafted or terrifyingly gargantuan that any lingering agnosticism can burn off as quickly as a morning's skiff of frost. The tremulous sense of vulnerability prepares us, as though we were a field being plowed, to gather "the fear of God."

We usually perceive our frailty during harrowing events such as catastrophe or disease. One minister in his sermons calls it "the hospital phenomenon"—the transformation he has seen his parishioners undergo upon finding themselves confined between a hospital's walls.

Buffeted by sickness and dread, conscious of medicine's limits, many turn—with a speed he as a young pastor found dizzying—to prayer.

All of us can cite examples of this in our own lives. But surely there is something heedless about waiting for disease or other crises to remind us how completely we rely on God. It is like the sailors in Shakespeare's *The Tempest* who cry out, "All lost! To prayers, to prayers! All lost!"

And this is where wilderness enters, for it is that rare arena where we encounter our limits, our precariousness, from a position of health rather than sickness. Wilderness can ignite prayer when we are upright on two feet in gratitude, not only when we are on our knees in despair.

But isn't there something artificial and contrived about this—deliberately seeking out our dependence on God? I don't think so. At least it strikes me as little different from taking part in the more common religious tradition of fasting. By breaking with the familiar, abstaining from customary comforts, both a sojourn and a fast can be efforts to define our human limitations, underscoring our proper relationship to God.

In both cases, the emotions felt, the prayers stirred, are no less genuine because we initiated the rapprochement. Perhaps it makes no difference to God how we come to him. But I can't help but think it's wiser to intentionally remind ourselves at intervals how absolute is our dependence, in advance of events that pummel us to the ground.

We remember suffering with distaste; the anguish may have been so wracking that we try to distance ourselves from everything involved in the incident, including the God we leaned upon—banishing from the mind, as C. S. Lewis wrote, "the only thing that supported me under the threat because it is now associated with the misery of those few days." A passage through wilderness may similarly illumine our mortality and transience, but the experience is distinct in one critical aspect. Instead of shrinking from the memory of our reliance on God, we anticipate recreating the experience, for it was born not in exhaustion but in something approaching exhilaration.

I round a corner of the canyon this morning and come face-to-face with another person. He is my age, also alone, and about to leave his camp and return upstream. We exchange pieces of information—locations of campsites and springs, weather predictions—and, in one of those conversations you can have with someone you'll never see again, we reminisce briefly over coffee about our childhoods. He mentions that when he was younger, his grandmother would call him every Sunday evening to ask whether he had been to church. Invariably he had been out hiking, but not wanting to disappoint her, he would reply that, yes, he had been to the Church of the Pines. She never asked its address and was pleased by his regular attendance.

From the "Church of the Pines" to the "Mount of the Holy Cross," visitors have christened the backcountry with scores of religious metaphors. John Muir's images are not uncommon: "As well dam for water-tanks the people's cathedrals and churches," he raged over the flooding of a pristine, Yosemite-like valley, "for no holier temple has ever been consecrated by the heart of man."

Curiously, however, those who affirm wilderness as spiritually invigorating seldom accord the same status to chapels of brick or steel. And, of course, vice versa: churchgoers often scoff at suggestions that wilderness can foster belief in anything save dryads.

And so those in the pines and those in the pews regard each other warily, discounting the legitimacy of the other's faith-kindling reservoir, each tending to see his sanctuary alone as the repository of God's glory.

I've been surprised by the number of pastors and lay-people I've met who tend to slight wilderness travel, dismissing it as "communing with nature," skeptical that any authentic religious sensibilities could be honed in the open air.

Some religious groups have been in the vanguard of those seeking to dismantle wild country, as if travel in such parts encouraged a dalliance with Pan. But more common are laity and clergy who regard wilderness with indifference, as a region useful only for the venting of excess energy by church youth groups. They seem to overlook the scriptural importance of wilderness—as a place of testing for the Hebrews, of solitude for the prophets, and of prayer for Jesus. Limiting wilderness to a sermon metaphor ("canyons of desolation," "deserts of despair"), clergy in particular neglect an arena that has nurtured faith for Desert Fathers, monastic orders, and contemporary pilgrims. Wilderness remains not merely a symbol but an actual setting—a spiritual reservoir able to evoke prayer as spontaneously as a house of worship built by human hands.

With the stream flowing so steadily to one side, I find it hard to imagine its absence. But this is the desert's abode; the stream is a guest. I once saw how quickly water could disappear—in another canyon, in another season. A friend and I had camped beside a spring, only to find it evaporated by morning. For a day we searched the canyon, uncovering nothing but basins of dust and pebbles. As we lumbered on, the land began to wither before us; our tongues seemed to have mummified. We ventured at last up a side tributary and near its end, under a ledge, we discovered a pool of clear, stone-cold water. We sat and drank for hours. Coursing through our bodies along with the water was gratitude—an overwhelming sense of thankfulness for this wilderness sustenance. When we later retold the story to acquaintances, however, we found ourselves speaking little of this gratefulness. We accented instead our perseverance, our ingenuity in turning up the right tributary. As soon as we left the desert behind, gratitude began to metamorphose into self-congratulation.

I have been walking for hours this morning, bend after bend, barely conscious of the scenery. Such a rhythmic pace, as walkers in any landscape can attest, allows thoughts to exhibit a curious agility. But a wilderness traveler has an additional advantage over a walker in the neighborhood woods: the *expectation* of unbroken silence. It is the unusual urban path that does not abruptly terminate at a development or road crossing, puncturing a thought, deflating a tentative insight. But here, the trail continues on, far longer than I could walk in a single day; my capacity to concentrate draws to an end well before the terrain does.

Late in the morning I stop at a spring to drink. Only as I finish the water do I become aware of the splash of wildflowers on the ground around me: yellow evening primroses, scarlet gilia, and, against the cliff, still in cool shadows, the datura's cream-white trumpet flowers.

I know the biological reasons for wildflowers. They provide a crucial part of the ecological chain: they offer food for insects; their roots, by breaking up rock, release nutrients while simultaneously anchoring fragile soil. But I can't help but think there are other reasons for them. These "lilies of the field" seem gratuitously bestowed, given in such abundance, as a manifestation of God's providence. The purest hues I have ever seen have been contained in wildflowers. They are a promise to us, these rainbow colors of the earth, as spiritually expressive as biologically so.

The day's geographical destination is a river in the wilderness. According to my map, it lies past a few more curls of the canyon. Around one bend, I see above me an alcove in the cliff—a fine setting to pass the upcoming night—so I leave my backpack in the sand and continue with little delay toward the river, walking faster now, pulled by anticipation. As I follow each meander, my exhiliration increases. So certain am I the next turn will open onto the river that I am barely conscious of the sculpted canyon and its lacquered stone.

After a half dozen curves reveal only more canyon walls, I begin to doubt the map's veracity; each twist becomes like a false summit that conceals the final destination. Just then, however, I round a bend to see the slender passageway suddenly flaring into an expanse of sunlight and sky.

For a moment I stand at the junction and let the canyon stream, muddied by my walking, filter clean; in seconds, the churned stream is transparent, merging imperceptibly with the river. From somewhere comes a salt breeze, as though the ocean were around the corner and not hundreds of miles distant.

This is more sky than I have seen in days—broad, blue, and unbroken by a cloud. The river too is wide, vast in comparison to the thin stream I have been following. I am bracketed by enormous wine-red cliffs that rise smooth and sheer up to the desert plateau.

For some time I don't move; I just stand there in the

shallow water feeling the river tugging at my ankles as it slides to the south. The afternoon sun glances off the river's surface, scattering colored light back into my eyes.

Perhaps it is the afternoon's stillness, or the convergence of stone and sky, but it seems to me as though no corner of the world could cup more water-spun serenity. I try to hold on to the moment, to take it back intact, but the sunlight shifts, and the wind picks up, and the moment is gone as though carried by the current away.

Near the canyon's mouth, I find an overhanging ledge where I eat a late afternoon lunch. Above me the first intrusion in days—a plane on a scenic expedition—crosses between the canyon walls. I wave, slowly, so they don't mistake my salutation for a distress signal: it would be difficult to discern my smile from two thousand feet.

I am not sorry to see the plane; the passengers can take in the canyon's serpentine elegance. Seen from above, it must appear like an improbably green tendril curling through the ocher desert. But the motor, as it splits the silence, is a reminder that other, less transitory, incursions are in the works for this wilderness: a dam has already begun to flood nearby canyons; a highway is being planned to blast through the sandstone where I am sitting. The wilderness that can instill such feelings of fragility in us is, itself, paradoxically fragile, able to be preserved or destroyed with the stroke of a pen.

I've been conscious in recent days of what wilderness does for us. But there is, of course, the other side: what do we, as stewards, do for wilderness? How much should be preserved? I once would have answered by simply weighing the secular value of wild country—its importance for recreation, psychological growth, and biological study.

But now I would add another consideration: what is the spiritual value of wilderness? What are our needs for these places of silence, solitude, and awe? More important, what will be our descendants' needs for them a century from now, in a world likely to be far more drained of contemplative reservoirs?

Wilderness is not sacrosanct; each acre everywhere need not be preserved. But there comes a time—and in this country it has been reached—when so few pockets of wild country survive that the spiritual values they harbor become worth more than the marketable commodities able to be extracted.

There are those who argue wilderness exists for its own sake, that it has intrinsic value apart from its importance to anyone or anything.

Others reply that wilderness exists for the benefit of humans—its timber, minerals, and water providing us with whatever we need; we may alter its profile however we choose.

But it seems wiser to me to assume that wilderness exists not for its own sake, nor for ours, but for God's

sake. Along with the rest of creation, it praises and wit-
nesses to his craftsmanship. God uses it as he wills—to
offer a source of regenerative soil and water, to provide
shelter for wild creatures, to bring humans closer in
prayer—or for untold other purposes that we may under-
stand but dimly.

But what of "subdue the earth"? Isn't there a biblical
mandate to cut and pave and trammel? At one time I
questioned the translation: surely, *subdue* was over-
wrought; a milder verb should be called for. But no solace
is to be found in these quarters. The original Hebrew
word is, if anything, even harsher in tone.

Some have argued that the injunction has been re-
pealed by events: extended before the Fall, it can no
longer be interpreted properly by humans. (Indeed, following the Flood, the commands of the first chapter of
Genesis are repeated to Noah—with the exception of
"subdue the earth.")

But what if the scriptural imperative still holds? Do no
restrictions or limitations apply? Are we obliged eventually to level the Matterhorn and irrigate the Sahara? These
are impractical if not impossible tasks, but, more important, the approach would seem heedless—seizing a single
phrase and wrenching it from a biblical context involving
an intricate set of relationships between God and the
natural world.

Wilderness has worked to bring humans to God; the
land has provided a refuge for listening and prayer. I read

of its reconciling biblical role, I know how it can affect contemporary sojourners who venture there, and I cannot believe that, as some contemporary critics have asserted, God intended no land be left in wilderness. It seems wiser to move with some prudence here, before irreversibly dismantling the few remnants of what has proven throughout history to be not only an ecological but a spiritual preserve.

In the evening I camp near the high alcove I glimpsed earlier on my way to the river. As night settles in, I start a driftwood fire, drying on upright stakes my socks, which are wet from the stream crossings I've made. By firelight I consume a quick meal: tuna fish from a can, crackers, lemons, and hot chocolate. Through the rift in the canyon walls, moonlight cascades down the cliff.

One mark of these wilderness retreats for me is their relative rarity; now, with a family, I am able to depart alone for the backcountry only once or twice a year. But what I have found essential is to be gone at least one night, for something disconcerting happens as I camp amid the land's unsettling rustlings: night falls and fractures my sense of security.

Near the town where I live there is a trail leading into the mountains. I've traveled it so often each bend is as well known to me as the town's main street. I've worn away the cusp of awe, and the trail is no longer wilderness to me. But everything can change if I spend a full night along its path. It is then, as the darkness blurs the outlines of familiar landscapes, that the wilderness at last begins to come into view.

The only footprints I've seen in the sand are those belonging to the fellow I encountered earlier. No one else seems to be in the canyon. Tonight, as in past evenings, I will hear no person's voice. The isolation makes me increasingly mindful of friends who are not here. The simple explanation: by this point in the stay I am beginning to ache for conversation and companionship. But there is another reason as well: wilderness tends to reconcile me with those who are absent. Disagreements shrink from this distance. Solitude puts into focus far more of my own faults than those of others. I am sure there are those who have gone to wilderness to feel a sense of defiant independence; but tonight I am more conscious not only of my need for God, but of my need for others—for family and friends.

It is one of the paradoxes of wilderness retreats, and perhaps all spiritual retreats: by withdrawing temporarily from others we can be brought closer to them.

It's curious how prayers change. In the early days, when I am preoccupied with my safety and the canyon's physical perils, they crackle like sparks from a wet fire. Only after time do prayers settle down, growing more steady and enduring, for there is another purpose to them. Less concerned with my own well-being, I am more conscious of the world I have left behind. This evening I read a parable from Matthew's Gospel—to feed the hungry, to provide water for the thirsty, to visit those in prison—and the familiar verse has seldom seemed more compelling. Here, deep in the desert where I am least able to respond, there is, ironically, perfect clarity of what must be done, and uninterrupted time to do it.

The wilderness is an improbable place to be haunted by a statistic, but there is one that keeps recurring to me: forty thousand children around the world die each day from disease. From measles, tetanus, diarrhea, pneumonia. Preventable diseases. Forty thousand children. Not each year, each day. I imagine myself as a parent, with no access to clean water or medicine, watching my child die.

And I find myself thinking: what am I doing here? I am helping no one; no child anywhere will go to bed in better health because of what I have done this day.

But what wilderness does do is to provide a perspective and a spur to conscience—what I must try to do when I return; how astonishingly little I contributed when I was there, only a few days before, within the human circle.

Tonight's fire hurls shadows hundreds of feet up the cliff. Some time ago, I sat beside another fire—this one in a hearth—as it snowed outside in late December. The topic of conversation was year-end reflective: what single event had most influenced us during the preceding twelve months?

I was uncertain at first how to respond. I had that year

graduated from law school, passed a bar exam, and moved to the Southwest. I had also taken my first trip alone into wilderness that autumn, and it was this event I found myself relating. I sketched the cliffs and wildflowers I had encountered. I mentioned the sense of fear and awe and, finally, for this was not a gathering that felt comfortable with such digression, I touched on prayer.

One contemporary author in his autobiography wrote that he would offer no account of a particular vacation because it was unimportant: the days could be taken out of his life and he would be absolutely no different as a person. It is simplistic to say that a wilderness sojourn never similarly trails off into irrelevance. But more often than not, these journeys reach our hearts, affecting us as deeply as any events we have ever undertaken. We depart for home not only with photographs and journals filled, but with a sense of divine initiative, and conscious of the initiative we must take ourselves.

FIFTH DAY

I slept deeply last night. I usually wake up a half dozen times, shifting ungracefully in my sleeping bag as I peer into the dark and recall where I am. But this morning I have even overslept. The belated start fits in well with the day. I've planned only a short walk up the river, then a return to this alcove by evening. My map promises long, looping meanders with crescent-shaped cliffs and, not far upstream, yet another tributary canyon. I'm looking forward to venturing into this companion cleft and tracing briefly its sinuous passage.

As I intend to return here tonight, there is no need to carry most of my belongings; I'll take with me only essentials of food, first aid, and water. I often feel some ambivalence about embarking on day hikes from deep in the wilderness, and this morning is no different. I am eager to probe new territory and stroll unburdened. But, at the same time, I am mindful of what stays behind here at camp. When I began the journey, provisions such as tent and sleeping bag seemed meager resources; now, as I leave them behind, I feel as though I've slipped from moorings in a safe port.

I look back at the alcove for a moment. My hesitation, such as it is, does not last long. The sun is high, the sky is blue, and the river is waiting.

When I step into the water, the chill takes my breath away. I am cloaked in sunshine, but the river only recently left cold shadows, and my feet protest as I walk upstream against the swift, shallow flow.

Cliffs, their sharp rims etched against the sky, fall for nearly a thousand feet to the river. To my side, sandbanks host a luxuriant mantle of green. Willows and lime-colored tamarisk trail their branches in the current. Cottonwood trees, having drunk for years from this watercourse, congregate on the banks in thick-trunked antiquity.

This is one of those mornings when I wish others were beside me, taking in the canyon plumage. I keep waiting to hear exclamations of delight over my shoulder.

Not long ago, in another part of the Southwest, a friend introduced me to his favorite cleft. We trudged across a flat unbroken expanse until suddenly, a few feet ahead of us, the sands parted. My friend watched gratified as I gazed with appreciation into the canyon's luminous upper reaches.

Traveling alone, I miss sharing those quickenings of breath. I often prefer the topography of solitude, but my maps are charted with places to return to someday with others.

I once attempted to graft together solitude and community. Several of us arranged to journey into the mountains on a silent retreat. We agreed to hike without conversing and eat our meals alone. On a summer afternoon, with the aspens green and the air effervescent, we began to walk. Rain showers passed through, only long enough to mist our faces and bestow a succession of double rainbows. The hike was exhilarating.

But the silence would not keep. We clustered together on the trail, starting half sentences, only to lapse back into awkward silence. The framework seemed foreign, and eventually it caved in on itself. We ate together, told stories, confided ambitions. I don't think any of us would exchange an hour of the memory. But silence and solitude proved harder to accept than we expected.

Camping in large groups I've encountered a similar effect in the evenings, when we've stood deciding where to spread our sleeping bags. The wilderness stretches out in all directions with its promise of yawning silence, but where do we chose to sleep? Side by side, or at no greater distance from each other than the sound of a snore. Even during slumber we tend to huddle together, circling our wagons against the unknown that presses in at nightfall.

Somehow I have missed the new canyon. I am far upstream from where I expected its confluence. My eyes have been sweeping the river's cliffs but the walls have yet to yield an opening.

Sitting down on a sandbar, I empty an hour's grit from my wet shoes. I lean back, rubbing my abraded feet, and look about me. I am not lost, but I feel disoriented. Anxieties seldom travel singly and before long I've startled up a covey of concerns. Surveying my feet I worry that they will be so chafed by day's end as to make further hiking painful. Overhead, I notice mare's tail clouds in the sky; the cirrus plumes seem often to foreshadow a weather change for the worse.

During backcountry trips, I can expect fretfulness to seep in at some point, souring the hours, and it is here now. If I look for worries, there is no end of them to vex my mind.

At home anxiety overtakes me more often than I care to admit. I imagine diverse misfortunes, as though all the scenarios not only could happen, but could occur simultaneously. I find myself praying for immunity from each contingency that could befall me and those I love.

"Do not be anxious," said Jesus. It's one of the hardest things I have to remember, here and elsewhere. I keep trying to use faith as if it were an amulet, forgetting that what Jesus promised was not security but presence.

My shoes rinsed of sand, I retrace my steps down the river. Around one oxbow meander I come upon a flock of dipper birds. Aptly named, they feed in the shallows, bobbing as if they were doing deep knee bends. I watch, fascinated, until they glimpse me and scatter toward the cliffs.

Following their flight, I notice a hairline crack in the sandstone. When I shift to one side, altering perspective, the crevice begins to open. I can see why I missed it before: the canyon greets the river at an upstream slant, its discreet entrance further concealed by thickets of alder and cottonwood.

In moments, I've moved past the vegetation and taken my first steps into the passage. The fissure quickly reveals its own signature. Walls seem darker here as they arch over me, the stone stained lavishly with desert varnish. The veneer of mineral oxide—leached from the rock by rainwater—streaks for hundreds of feet, as though burgundy and chestnut dyes had poured copiously down the cliff facade.

The canyon itself is dry; no slender stream coils along its path. I strain to listen, and the river behind me has become inaudible. I have walked back into the desert's hush.

Those who venture below the ocean return to tell of coral and colors invisible from the surface. So it is in this landscape. Someone traveling today across the Southwest might glance across the desert plateau and have little idea that these clefts are here, that just below the surface are roofless galleries of painted stone and light. Canyons are the desert's sunken vessels, submerged in sand rather than sea.

Whenever I enter wilderness, I am struck by the difference between being here in the open air and recalling it in words. From a distance, I tend to treat desert, forest, and mountain as abstractions—something to extol to others rather than to visit myself. I begin to overlook John Muir's advice: "To get these glorious works of God into yourself—that's the thing; not to write about them!" I'm startled at how easily I could let memories of wilderness suffice, neglecting my own periodic need to return here on retreat.

A friend takes issue, however, with the word *retreat.* If, he asks, the experience provides an antidote to spiritual inertia, if it can lessen estrangement from God, then isn't *retreat* a misnomer? He proposes instead *advance* or *approach.*

The words may border on presumption, but one dares to hope he's right. And so we continue on, wobbling forward on our spiritual approach.

This canyon curls more suddenly than the one that led me to the river; in places I can see only a few feet ahead. For one narrow stretch, stones cobble the sand, and when I step on them, they roll together like billiards, their clicks echoing hollowly off the cliffs.

As I walk, my mind turns for a moment to home, to preoccupations of work and ambition. Some of my concerns seem healthy and caring; more than a few are simply bedrock cravings for prestige and glory.

Vanities don't shrivel away in the wilderness, but they appear less alluring in the coruscating light. Here I glimpse their emptiness rather than their enchantment— the possibility they will prove more of a cul-de-sac than any box canyon encountered in this landscape.

British writer Malcolm Muggeridge found that for him in the wilderness, "all the habitual pursuits of the ego and appetites are suspended. . . . No social life, no media, no occasion for bitterness or frustration."

Elsewhere a frenetic pace enables me to camouflage myself; staying busy I don't have time to evaluate my pursuits. The setting here strips away that disguise and leaves me, and my strivings, exposed.

No shortage of sunshine today. The hot bronze light slices into the fissure, singeing away patches of shade. As I have on recent days, I recall a phrase from preacher Harry Emerson Fosdick. "Atheism is not our greatest danger, but a shadowy sense of God's reality." Not so much disbelief as uncertainty—a gray half-light, a sense of distance and alienation.

If some of the shadows melt away in wilderness, it is not because we encounter God exclusively here, as though one could predict the parameters of divinity. The significance of desert and mountain is not who resides here, but what we ourselves have left behind in coming.

I walk for only another quarter hour or so, and then rest on a boulder. I'm breathing more heavily than in younger years. On a recent backpacking trip, ascending a mountain pass, it dawned on me how the landscape had altered over time: what used to be a kilometer had stretched to a mile.

I sit for some time, unmoving and listening. Not a sound in the canyon. If conversion takes place during retreats, it seems not so much a snapping to, as the compass point jumps unerringly toward north. Here in wilderness, as in other sanctuaries of stillness, the change appears more measured. Some flowers are heliotropic, reorienting their position as they seek the sun. Their pace parallels our own. Like plants bending toward light, we turn, ever so slowly in silence and solitude, toward God.

I drink from a half-empty canteen; my other one is already dry. I've barely carried enough water. The canyon no doubt continues to furrow invitingly through the desert, each turn disclosing new palettes of desert varnish, but I feel as though I've gone far enough.

Over my shoulder, I see a shelf on the cliff and, higher still, a notched pour-off. During storms, water would funnel through the notch and splash on the shelf. If past rains have left water anywhere in the canyon, that is where it would be, in a basin pummeled out over time.

On an impulse, I grasp some handholds and pull myself up to the shelf. I feel a sudden thrill of confirmation: there is indeed a basin, still trapping water. Though not the most enticing liquid, it could slake thirst for weeks.

Just as I seize the thought that I am the first person to discover this hidden cistern, I glance up to see a stack of firewood beside the water, piled as neatly as if it were next to a hearth.

Who did this? Who would have used this shelf, with its gathered wood for cold nights and water for hot days?

The Anasazi Indians—the "Ancient Ones," ancestors of today's Pueblo Indians—traversed this watershed a thousand years ago, but the wood doesn't appear that weathered. A cattleman or miner of this century? Possibly a young poet who reputedly vanished in these canyons during the 1930s?

There are no clues, no initials or scratchings in the rock, only the firewood's mute testimony. This often happens to me in wilderness, chancing upon legacies of man and nature: I'm left with intimations without answers. Sometimes what I see here with my eyes is more enigmatic than what I take on faith.

Early in the afternoon, I turn back toward my camp. The canyon still pulsates with heat, and a faint breeze does little to whisk it away.

On day trips like this one, I often set down lists on a notepad. Some thoughts are prosaic (letters to send, articles to write), others more profound—touching on relationships, on amends to make or promises to keep. I dash the insights down hastily before they're lost, as single words and broken sentences. Halting in midstep, cupping the notepad, I write away feverishly, like a forlorn reporter interviewing the wind.

Many of these perceptions clamor for attention, but they can't be implemented here in the desert. That is an advantage: I've nothing to distract me from listing them, my notepad swelling with accretions of insight. But what I've found is that the urgency dissipates by the time I return home. A chasm exists between my initial glimpse and my response. It is as though I were standing high on one side of the canyon's rim, clutching my insights, looking across to where I wanted to be, separated by the thin air of inaction.

A friend who has backpacked widely speaks ruefully of this gulf between recognition and response. She first sensed it elsewhere, when she worked in a small town in Latin America. At the time, she was grappling with marital problems and conflicts with people at work. One day an earthquake struck, and she ran to the relative safety of a garden plaza as buildings shattered and dust billowed. "For those moments I saw everything so clearly," she recalls. "How I could become so much kinder to my husband, how other relationships could work out. In an instant—and with such gratitude—I saw how it would be so easy for me to turn things around."

When the tremors ceased, some of the clarity dimmed. But she had glimpsed how brokenness might be mended. Her vision was, as it can be in wilderness, not accusatory —not a blaming of others—but of what she herself could do to heal, and the burden for change subtly shifted.

The canyon floor may be bone dry, but its appearance is deceiving. Storms could turn this passageway into wall-to-wall water, twenty feet deep. Lest I have any doubt about its ability to metamorphose, I see, on ledges above me, jagged trunks of trees bequeathed by past flash floods.

In the Sermon on the Mount, Jesus cautioned those who heard his teachings but did not respond. He compared such folly to building a house on sand rather than rock. For years I visualized the parable's stage as a beach washed by ocean tides. A more probable setting, one vividly familiar to Jesus' listeners, would have been Palestine's dry ravines—the *wadis*—that so closely resemble the Southwest's canyons and arroyos.

Not until I walked in this landscape did the parable's imagery become distressingly graphic. I saw the dry, level floor of ravines, the temptation to build, without foundations, in the sand. The edifice would stand splendidly until, as the parable notes, "the rain fell and the floods came." Then, not without warning, the channel would shudder and fill with a deluge that would dash everything in its path. And, as master builders, all we would be left with is a ruin of regret.

At the canyon's end I see the river ahead; at first I'm inclined to remain on the banks, but the sun is warm and my skin well caked by dust. With little hesitation, I wade into the shallows and stretch out, nearly immersed, as water glides past my ears.

Turning to one side, I see cottonwood trees in the afternoon's slanting light. Each leaf shimmers as if somehow lit from within. Below the cottonwoods' branches, dark grass stretches toward the cliff. Normally in this parched country, I'd encounter a few yellowing wisps of grass, but beside the river it bursts into an emerald-green expanse.

I once considered "streams in the desert" only a metaphor—an image of yearning, a promise of comfort. But streams in the desert do indeed flow, threading through the landscape, quenching and providing.

My clothes dry in the afternoon sun as I follow the river back to the alcove. This watercourse is too shallow to raft, but I've floated other rivers nearby, watching canyon country unscroll at the current's chosen pace.

Each river has revealed tiers of rapids, and in rafting them there is always a moment when the boat is poised on the lip of the white water, suspended in time, and beyond that mark, there is no turning back. We slide inexorably into turbulence, surging past sinkholes and boulders, until we reach smooth water on the far side.

I will soon return home to challenges, deadlines, and stress—what I've come to call the rapids in my own life. The stretches of white water are often exhilirating; I've entered many of them willingly. But at times the rapids follow one another relentlessly, and once swept into the throes, I've lost any chance to reflect or reconsider. Caught in the current, engulfed in the roar, I look to the side and see weeks of my life moving past in a blur. The only time to pull to shore, I've learned belatedly, is when you hear the rapids approaching.

When I reach my campsite in the alcove, little light remains, and I make preparations for dinner. Simple foods, with no pans to wash save a cup for soup.

The night air is clear and, as in recent evenings, free of insects. I sometimes forget how unusual this is. A New England friend confesses that mosquitos can be an insurmountable distraction. ("Too many bugs," he says, "and

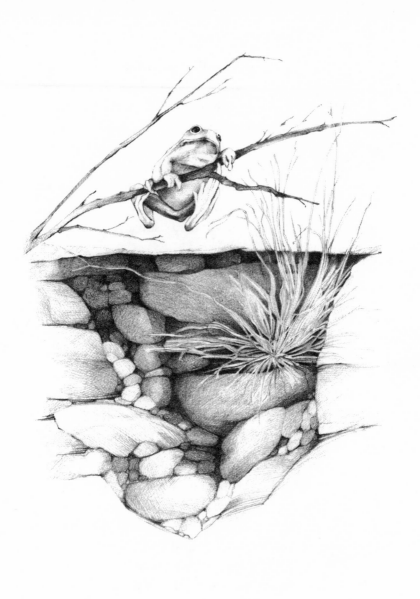

I start slapping irritably and any contemplative moment is lost.")

I empathize with him. It takes a different temperament than mine to welcome black flies and gnats, so I try to come here in seasons when they are scarce. The decision reflects a broader deference I give wilderness by not wandering in during extremes. I know people who've cheerfully left for deserts at summer's zenith and mountains on the eve of monsoons. For less hardy souls, there's a timing to these visits.

One need not travel far. To gather the benefits of wild lands, it is not necessary to bushwhack to the most remote cavern or inhospitable crag. I haven't found a correlation between spirituality and the number of miles walked. Quiet, contemplative qualities thrive as well on the more accessible periphery of wilderness. The retreat's purpose, after all, is to reconnoiter contours that are more spiritual than physical.

My friend looks bewildered when I speak of intangible values encountered in wilderness. "Encountered *where?*" she asks doubtfully. We are accustomed to hearing of wild lands as arenas for conquest and adventure, not as settings for reflection. "Contemplative" wilderness strikes an incongruous sound. For the most part, the spiritual offering of the backcountry remains startlingly unexpected, as much terra incognita as the land itself.

Spiritual values have not always been in such eclipse. During early efforts to preserve the country's wilderness, conservationists unabashedly heralded such qualities as silence, solitude, and awe. Author Sigurd Olson noted that spiritual values were "the real reason for all the practical things we must do to save wilderness. In the last analysis it is the spiritual values we are really fighting to preserve."

Some conservationists spoke from a religious tradition; others from an ethical framework. But all prized wilderness as a counterbalance to hubris. As naturalist Howard Zahniser counseled, "Our emphasis in wilderness should be our humility rather than our dominance."

But in recent years, spiritual values have fallen from the constellation of reasons for protecting wild lands. Other traditional rationales—recreational, ecological, economic—have displaced the less quantifiable aspects of wild country with charts, visitor-use graphs, and cost-benefit analyses.

We seem increasingly uncomfortable speaking of spiritual qualities, as if their intangibility rendered them inauthentic. And so we abandon language able to describe not only the heart of wilderness, but the recesses of our own hearts.

Late evening. The canyon's vesper light has given way to darkness. Warmth, however, lingers for a while, and I sit in the sand and lean against my backpack. Not yet sleepy, I read by flashlight some pages from C. S. Lewis.

One paragraph touches on our attempt to find something other than God that will make us eternally happy. Lewis suggests the effort is in vain: "God designed the human machine to run on Himself. . . . God cannot give us a happiness and peace apart from Himself, because it is not there."

Similar echoes come down the centuries: Pascal's perception that we have a God-shaped hollow within us that only God can fill. And from Augustine, "Our hearts are restless til they find rest in Thee."

The canyon is getting colder. I take a last sip of water from the canteen. From other settings it is possible to dismiss such comments as merely clever aphorisms. Not this evening, not from this posture in the desert.

When I pray tonight, I say the prayers aloud. I seldom give voice to them, and the utterance startles me, in part because these are the first words I've heard in days. I am conscious of how slight my voice is here under the stars; no resonance or echo. The words simply disappear into the night. But not before bridging, as prayers everywhere seem to do, heaven and earth in a soundless span.

SIXTH DAY

I remain in my sleeping bag later than usual this morning. I slept poorly last night; it took some time to drift off, and I fell into a restless sleep only to awaken near midnight. The moon had climbed high and drenched the canyon in silver half-light. As I rose on one elbow, I saw the figure of an animal nosing the ground next to me. It was a ringtail cat, its huge curling tail diaphanous in the moonlight. I lay still at first, uncertain whether this was some relic from my unsettled rest, but when I muttered a few words aloud, it looked up at me. Separated by only a few feet, we stared unwaveringly into each other's eyes. Then, as the moon was enclosed by a tumult of black clouds, it slowly turned and padded away into the night.

I've seen few wild creatures so closely; most have been mere specters—the hindquarters of a bear, the shadow of a mountain lion—sightings so quick and tentative that I wondered whether I had seen anything at all. But as seldom as they are glimpsed, the wild animals sharpen the edge of our awe. Each creature—aside from existing as part of God's creation and the rich network of life—serves to rein in our sense of self-mastery. "We need to witness our own limits transgressed," as Thoreau once wrote, "and some life pasturing freely where we never wander."

The canyon is cool this morning. The sun has yet to crest the walls and flood this stone atrium. The temperature will soon soar, but now I unfurl myself from the sleeping bag, pull on a wool cap, and quickly dress.

A brief breakfast, the customary wilderness morning meal: coffee, a fresh orange, homemade oatmeal cookies. The last is a gracious parting gift from my wife, Deborah, who looks upon these annual wilderness sojourns with mixed feelings. For her own retreats she chooses something closer to home—a Benedictine monastery in northern New Mexico, set beside a river. Though not Catholic, she prefers the silent fellowship and communion of that place apart which, in the Desert Fathers' tradition of hospitality, has opened its doors to retreatants.

She is disinclined to visit wild country alone, but she acknowledges that others feel differently, and so she guardedly approves of these few days I spend in wilderness. And sends her prayers.

This morning I have begun the return walk up the canyon, back toward the car I left so many miles ago. I am in the same passageway that brought me to the river, but now, as I change directions, the canyon at times assumes an unfamiliar countenance. I see things from this angle I missed entirely on my way down—sandstone arches and deep jade pools and, in the late morning, something else: a cliff dwelling perched high on a canyon ledge.

At first I think it is simply debris from an ancient flash flood. But a second glance convinces me I am looking not at mud but at mortar—a prehistoric stone house with walls and windows. After a few moments, I can even discern spindly roof beams protruding beyond the alcove.

I work my way over to the cliff and begin an ascent up a series of narrow terraces. But before long, I am stymied: the final ledges leading to the cliff dwelling have been sheared away with time. The house, preserved for the past millennium in the dry desert air, will remain inaccessible to me.

On the shelf where I stand lie pieces of buff-colored pottery and burnt ears of corn. I have seen ancient potsherds and corncobs before—behind glass-fronted exhibits in museums. But here, displayed in the open air where they have lain for centuries, their effect on me is overpowering. I think of the last person to eat this corn, to hold the pottery, and the passage of time—and my own sojourning status—has never been so disconcertingly brought home to me.

Usually in the backcountry it is the imposing terrain that humbles so well. But at times it can be something small and man-made—these potsherds, for example, or rusting tools in a weed-choked cabin—that instills in wilderness visitors a nearly unbearable sense of transience.

And here on the ledge, in the full flush of morning light, I come face-to-face with St. James's counsel: "For what is your life? It is even a vapour, that appeareth for a little time, and then vanisheth away."

I lean against the cliff and look along the canyon's length. From this modest aerie I can see the passage twisting away in both directions. The river lies a half day's walk behind me; my car and the roadway home are a long day's walk ahead. The weather seems to be holding; today the sky is cloudless.

I know a woman who calls prayer "a lovely desert plant that thrives in the wilderness." More common are those friends who've never associated wilderness with prayer. I spent scores of nights under the stars before I had an inkling that the country offered more than picturesque landscape. Something else was happening here, something that promised to alter how I viewed my relationship to God. I'm not sure if anything but the outlines of that pride-splintering sense of vulnerability would have been apparent to me had I not entered the wilderness, at long last, alone.

By accident a friend became lost. He was traveling with a dozen companions through a broad, meandering canyon filled with shrubs, and by chance he got ahead of his friends. The others, assuming he was behind, slowed down to wait. He, certain his companions would be walking faster than he was, increased his pace. By dusk they were stretched out miles apart. Night fell and instead of the comforting sounds of dinners being prepared around him, all my friend heard was the echo of his voice against towering cliff walls. He had stumbled into solitude. He was more isolated than he had ever been, adrift in a desert

of silence and stars. Later, he would not talk about the experience except to say this: "It was terrifying. The best night of the trip."

We read books about the importance of solitude. How to practice it so that it nurtures and mends. We concur with theologian Henri Nouwen when he describes solitude as the "furnace of transformation." We embrace Thomas Merton's observation that "as soon as you are really alone you are with God." And what it comes down to is that most of us find it easier to read about solitude than to practice it.

Moreover, when we admit it to ourselves, there is a stigma attached to being alone. Solitude, often seen as a twilight province of eccentrics and misanthropes, is suspect. This social taint, as much as the specter of danger, works to discourage solitary excursions into the wilderness. We hear of acquaintances who have gone alone for a few days to the desert or mountain, and our first response is likely to be a solicitous query: "What's wrong with them?"

Not long ago, author and environmentalist David Brower asked his readers: "How long were you ever altogether alone in all your life?" He replied that, for himself, the answer would be some thirty hours, years ago when he was a young man.

I've asked this question of friends and the immediate response tends to be, "Of course I've been alone, often, when traveling in cities where I've known no one for days."

But when the question is clarified ("altogether alone") the reply takes longer. Rarely have I heard an answer of more than twenty-four hours.

The experience of prolonged solitude, voluntarily chosen, is rare. It should not be surprising that few of us pass time by ourselves in the wilderness; we seldom seek out solitude anywhere.

My reverie is broken by a lizard glinting across the sandstone, and I begin to climb down from the ledge. The descent is always more troubling than the ascent, and I slip at one point, cutting a finger. While putting on a bandage, I briefly chronicle my other ailments: blisters on one foot; cactus-scraped knees; a sunburnt face. Travel in the canyons can begin to erode a visitor, leaving one as weathered as the strata.

My body at last is becoming adjusted to the backpack. Each morning as I put it on, my shoulders are sore, but within minutes I'm barely mindful of the weight; the pack has become an extension of me. As I feel more comfortable in the canyon, I begin to shift my focus to the future. I've always brought concerns that are bothering me into the wilderness. Here under a desert sun, where life seems glaringly precarious, priorities become clear. The most important decisions I have made—on how I would live my days—have occurred in the wilderness when I was alone.

The word *wilderness* is often used to suggest restricted sight, and indeed, in one sense this is so: I can see only a few yards ahead before the canyon twists out of view; the cliffs overhead rise so high they squeeze the sky to a bare filament of blue. Yet, in another sense, perhaps nowhere is the perspective more open than from here. Cloistered by solitude and encompassed by silence, I've worked my way past tumultuous terrain, to emerge in a clearing where I can see for years.

Beware, a friend of mine cautioned me not long ago. Don't overdramatize the salutary effects of wilderness solitude: some people entering wilderness expectantly will encounter only boredom or paralyzing fear. And he had a point. At times, a wilderness journey leads to no moments of insight or prayer that we can take back with us; we are too busy keeping dry or warm or safe to see beyond the next few minutes. We struggle home from the wilderness dampened and dispirited, feeling further from God than before we left.

But a more common experience is to avoid going in the first place. To say that there are needs that must be met at home. To say, even when vacations or weekends are unplanned, that the backcountry is too distant or inconvenient. For the most part, such reasoning becomes an insurmountable hurdle. And so wilderness remains out of reach, and we go about our business down through the years.

An elderly couple I know treat wildflowers as others might veins of gold. They fall upon primroses and penstemons with cries of delight, faithfully recording each discovery in letters dispatched to their children.

They are both over seventy years old. They began walking in wilderness when they retired. I think of them —and their brisk hiking pace—when I hear that backcountry travel is only for the young. People of all ages are venturing into forest, desert, and mountains. Wilderness travel, by foot or horseback, is one of the country's fastest growing recreations; few journeys from home can be as inexpensive. Programs designed for those with handicaps, as well as for individuals from the inner city, have made wild country accessible to many heretofore unable to visit. The decision to pass time in wilderness is increasingly a matter of interest rather than solely a question of age or endurance.

When I read works by Christian contemplatives who have lived in the desert or who have drawn on the sayings of the early Desert Fathers, I am struck by how consistently they convert *wilderness* into a figure of speech. They assume that, for others, the country itself is wholly inaccessible—being too hot or cold, too distant or perilous— and they urge that we do the best we can by making our deserts at home, setting aside corners of stillness to withdraw to regularly.

We nod, agreeing with their advice; we readily acknowledge the need to carve out contemplative niches, and then, for the most part, do not do so. "Too many worthy activities, valuable things, and interesting people," as Anne Morrow Lindbergh once observed. "For it is not merely the trivial which clutters our lives but the important as well." Unable to make time for silence and solitude, we catch a glimmer of a twentieth-century irony: figurative deserts becoming more remote and inaccessible than actual ones.

In the late afternoon, I make camp in the shade of a cliff. Above me, the wall is burnt orange as it catches the last of the sun. I am only a few miles from my car; the distance can be easily covered tomorrow morning.

Sitting beside the stream, I write down a paradox of wilderness travel. Here, along with the humbling awe I've felt since the first afternoon, are occasional flashes of self-mastery. I find myself reveling at times in the knowledge that I've made the journey alone, without others. I've survived, even prospered: I am as healthy, certainly leaner, possibly wiser than when I entered the canyon. I've wrestled with solitude, altering my beliefs in my physical and psychological limits.

For these moments, I overlook not only dependence on God but my material debt to others—individuals who grew the food I've been eating, who sewed the tent that shelters me, who made the sleeping bag that still, after twenty years of use, keeps me warm at night. I am tied umbilically to others. I could not have made this journey by myself. The danger of wilderness solitude is not so much the visible perils unique to these halls of stone, but rather the same danger that is everywhere: pride that says I've come this far by myself.

In the evening I eat dinner by firelight and feel my body responding to the nourishment, exhaling weariness. The wilderness is a place of rest—not in the sense of being motionless, for the lure, after all, is to move, to round the next bend. The rest comes in the isolation from distractions, in the slowing of the daily centrifugal forces that keep us off balance.

For a few days we withdraw to orient ourselves, sojourning in a land where the risk is not so much of being lost as being found. "Come ye yourselves apart into a desert place," said Jesus, "and rest a while."

Whenever I enter the wilderness accompanied by friends, I find an evening when I leave the campsite behind and, for an hour or so, walk alone along the trail. It is a hard thing to do, this leaving others, when one has come in a group and camped together for days. As they stay and I go, the fragile bonds of companionship are briefly frayed.

But alone, I walk more slowly, unhurried by other footsteps; my concentration is unbroken by conversation. For the first time in days, the delicate and shy become apparent: a sinuous whorl of peach-colored sandstone; the silver filigree of a spiderweb; faded prints of bighorn sheep in the sand. In the stillness, I recall a quickly forgotten lesson: so many things can only be *seen* in silence.

Christians have a rich tradition of leaving behind, in St. Gregory's words, "the clamor of earthly activity" to live in nature's more secluded corners: the early Desert Fathers of Egypt and Palestine; the *poustiniks* of Russia's forests and deserts; hermits and monks in nearly every country of the world.

But often they have separated themselves for years, if not a lifetime. The withdrawal has become a vocation. But why hasn't a modification of this arisen—entering the wilderness not to dwell but to sojourn—patterned on Jesus' own brief withdrawals throughout his ministry?

Those who have sequestered themselves in wilderness have still looked out—offering not simply prayer for the world but tangible aid. The Desert Fathers extended hospitality to strangers; the solitary Russian *poustiniks* heeded calls for help from neighboring villages. We tend to think of hermits as churlishly detached, isolation having bred both alienation and rancor. But for these pilgrims, the destination has not been wilderness but God; the desert passage has softened the heart into compassion and repentance. And that process, it seems to me, can begin after a few hours as well as after long years.

Near my camp slopes a gentle slab of sandstone, still warm from the sun's long arc, and for a while I lie back against it and watch the evening sky shade into a lavender dusk. Tomorrow I leave and return home. In the scented desert air, I can imagine staying, living here deep in the wilderness.

But it is a delusion. I could not remain. I am tied to the world, to people, and gratefully so. Moreover, there are things to do. Carlo Carretto, a member of the Catholic order The Little Brothers of Jesus, made clear his priorities as he wrote from the Sahara: "But the desert is not the final stopping place. It is a stage on the journey. . . . Our vocation is contemplation in the streets. . . . Certainly it would be easier and more pleasant to stay here in the desert. But God doesn't seem to want that."

And so we gather up these contemplative gifts of silence, solitude, and awe, and return, well laden, home.

SEVENTH DAY

My last morning in the canyon. I finish remnants of both the oatmeal cookies and coffee. The weather is changing; gray clouds have begun to scuttle across the desert sky. An uncommonly strong morning breeze stirs down the canyon, drifting grains of sand into my coffee. A good morning to be leaving.

I slept well last night, my body at last becoming adjusted to the curves of the earth. A friend of mine, after camping, returns home to sleep on his hardwood floor before making a transition to his bed. I, however, will accede immediately to a mattress. Indeed, the prospect of clean sheets and a roof over my head seems ineffably luxurious; the modest privations of the past few days have made me yearn for amenities I usually take for granted at home.

Lifting my backpack, I continue up the canyon, my footprints in the wet sand set alongside those I made earlier, pointing the other direction. Each tread, making a precise mold, promises to endure in this canyon. At least, that is, until the next rain, when a rising stream will smooth away the traces of anyone's having ventured into this corridor of time.

The argument that wilderness should be preserved for its natural beauty is bound to fail with those who perceive beauty not in crags or deserts but in tilled fields and landscaped parks; aesthetics is a slender reed on which to rest the case for preservation.

But if those same individuals recognize another dimension to wilderness—that it is part of the geography of faith, that it can kindle a profound sense of our dependence on God—then will they give the land a second look? Little time remains to persuade. In the next few years, those now living will choose the final parameters of this spiritual legacy for all coming generations.

In the town I will be returning to there is a garden, one often filled with tourists seeking a refuge from the city's heat. Roses, tulips, and columbine flourish around a central courtyard. One part of the ground has been given over to Oriental poppies and when they are in bloom, in the spring, that corner is on fire—the poppies' orange crepe-paper heads flaming up against an evergreen hedge. I walk along the brick paths, past rows of geraniums, and I express a certain gratitude. To whom? To the gardener for his skill in orchestrating this annual crescendo. (A gruff, white-haired man, he nods and accepts the praise.) But I find my appreciation stops with him. In the manicured garden it takes a clearer eye than mine to see past man's artistry to God's.

And that is the critical distinction between wilderness and the tamer, pastoral landscape of gardens and parks.

All nature may offer hints of God's handiwork, but only in wilderness do we not risk misdirecting ultimate praise; in wild country we are reminded, unequivocally and tremulously, who it is that made the earth.

I harbor a hope of hearing one day, particularly during sermons, the word *wilderness* used other than as a metaphor for gloom, bafflement, and personal crises. It is employed so relentlessly as a pejorative figure of speech, as a condition from which to extricate ourselves as soon as possible. Forgotten is the paradoxical biblical role of desert and mountain—to heal as well as humble, to reconcile as well as reproach—and the possibility that, on occasion, "in the wilderness" is precisely where we should choose to be journeying.

In the final few miles I will be passing a number of side tributaries with their secluded inner world of vertical cliffs and secret gardens. As I hiked past earlier on my way downstream, I told myself I would visit them on the way out. But today I feel little desire to explore; the momentum is to walk, to return, to make telephone calls announcing I am well, to sit at table with others. My prayers reflect a resurgence of concern for my safety. I move with exaggerated caution, anxious that no injury befall me so near to the end.

I see the opening of a cleft to my left. The tributary is dark and slender, with sheer vermillion walls. A stream issues from its portals, joining with the watercourse I've been following. I can see only a few yards into the crack before it swings enticingly around a sudden bend.

Next time, I tell myself. Next time.

And when will the next time be? To leave home, to set aside a few days is becoming no easier for me to do. When wilderness is most essential—when I long for its fluent silence—any leave-taking from family or job seems impossible.

Like Paul, who, after his Damascus road conversion, went "not to Jerusalem" but rather into the desert, we need the arena at critical junctures. More often than not, however, we are unable to plan ahead; we go when we can. Not, perhaps, to change directions abruptly, but simply to orient ourselves, gauging how far from course we've strayed.

The morning is still young when I begin to leave the canyon behind. The walls become shallower with each bend, and before long I am coming out on the desert plateau. With the sun not yet high, long blue shadows finger across the expanse of sagebrush and sandstone. I walk for some time until, far in the distance, I can see my car, the sun glinting off its roof through the cottonwood trees. I stop for a moment and turn around, but behind me now there is no hint of the canyons where I have spent the past days; the land appears to stretch out seamlessly in all directions.

Once I emerge from the wilderness, how can I remember the sense of utter dependence on God? The Hebrews, on leaving the Sinai, were told to carry a portion of manna with them as a reminder of God's providence. Moses, knowing what lay ahead, warned them: take heed, lest you forget; when you enter this new land and leave the wilderness, you will begin to think your hands have accomplished these things.

After forty years in the desert, the Hebrews could not remain steadfast. With our minor sojourns, how can we hope to remember? We take photographs of the landscape, we fill journals with notes, but photographs fade and words are soon misplaced. The problem is less with grasping a theological truth in the windswept solitude, than in holding on to it.

And so we return home, to family, to community, to the needs of the city. But the wilderness abides, and we will return here someday as well. We think of biblical wilderness as an arena to pass through only once. But Jesus returned. The prophets returned. Hosea would have had the entire nation return.

Someday in the future we will return. To gather our spiritual bearings; to grow in the silence and solitude; to feel the contours of fear and grace. And to recall who is God and who we are and what God would have us do.

SOURCES

PAGE NO.

    30   "The Earth is" Ps. 24:1.

    32   "And he withdrew" Luke 5:16.

    32   "And . . . he went" Luke 6:12.

    32   "And when he" Matt. 14:23.

    32   "And in the" Mark 1:35. (Or, as related in Luke 4:42, "And when it was day, he departed and went into a desert place.")

    33   "I will lift" Ps. 121: 1–2.

    35   "Be still, and" Ps. 46:10.

    36   "You see, what" C. S. Lewis, *Mere Christianity* (New York: Macmillan, 1943), 135–136.

FOURTH DAY

    42   "the fear of" Ps. 111:10.

    43   "All lost! To" William Shakespeare, *The Tempest* I, i, 48.

    44   "the only thing" C. S. Lewis, *The Problem of Pain* (New York: Macmillan, 1962), 106–107.

    45   "As well dam" John Muir, quoted by Roderick Nash, *Wilderness and the American Mind,* 3d. ed. (New Haven: Yale University Press, 1982), 168.

    52   "subdue the earth" Gen 1:28.

FIFTH DAY

    62   "Do not be" Matt. 6:25–34.

    63   "To get these" John Muir, quoted by Edwin Way

PAGE NO.

Teale, *The Wilderness World of John Muir* (Boston: Houghton Mifflin Co., 1976), xiii.

64 **"all the habitual"** Malcolm Muggeridge, *A Twentieth Century Testimony* (Nashville, Toronto, New York: Thomas Nelson, 1978).

65 **"Atheism is not"** Harry Emerson Fosdick, "The Sense of God's Reality" in *The Christian Century*, July 4–11, 1984, 677 (Reprinted from the November 6, 1919, issue).

69 **"the rain fell"** Matt. 7:24–27.

73 **"the real reason"** Sigurd Olson, "The Spiritual Need," in Bruce Kilgore, ed., *Wilderness in a Changing World* (San Francisco: Sierra Club, 1966), 212.

73 **"Our emphasis in"** Howard Zahniser, quoted in David Brower, ed., *Wildlands in Our Civilization* (San Francisco: Sierra Club, 1964), 164.

74 **"God designed the"** C. S. Lewis, *Mere Christianity* (New York: Macmillan, 1943), 54.

74 **"Our hearts are"** Augustine, *Confessions*, Book 1, Chapter 1, in *The Nicene and Post-Nicene Fathers*, vol. 1 (Grand Rapids, MI: Eerdmans, 1974), 45.

SIXTH DAY

77 **"We need to"** Henry David Thoreau, *Walden* (New York: New American Library, 1960), 211.

79 **"For what is"** James 4:14.

82 **"furnace of transformation"** Henri Nouwen, *The Way of the Heart* (New York: The Seabury Press, 1981), 25.

PAGE NO.

82 **"as soon as"** Thomas Merton, *Thoughts in Solitude* (New York: Farrar, Straus and Giroux, 1956), 113.

82 **"How long were"** David Brower, "Individual Freedom in Public Wilderness," *Not Man Apart,* May 1976, 2.

87 **"Too many worthy"** Anne Morrow Lindbergh, *Gift from the Sea* (New York: Pantheon, 1955), 115.

88 **"Come ye yourselves"** Mark 6:31.

89 **"the clamor of"** quoted in the *New Catholic Encyclopedia* vol. 12 (Washington, D.C.: Catholic University of America, 1967), 428.

90 **"But the desert"** Carlo Carretto, *Letters from the Desert* (Maryknoll, NY: Orbis, 1972), 74–75.

SEVENTH DAY

96 **"not to Jerusalem"** Gal. 1:17.